Here's all the great literature in this grade level of *Celebrate Reading!*

EAT UP, GEMMA

Written by
Sarah Hayes

Illustrated by
Jan Ormerod

The Doorbell Rang
by Pat Hutchins

When the
Elephant
Walks

Keiko Kasza

BOOK A
Under My Hat

Mary Had a Little Lamb
by Sarah Josepha Hale
Photographs by
Bruce McMillan
✳ ALA NOTABLE ILLUSTRATOR

Tickle-Toe Rhymes
from the collection by
Joan Knight
✳ PARENTS' CHOICE

Old Hat, New Hat
by Stan and Jan Berenstain
✳ MICHIGAN YOUNG READER
AWARD AUTHORS

So Can I
by Allan Ahlberg
✳ CHILDREN'S BOOK AWARD AUTHOR

**What Shall We Do
When We All Go Out?**
Illustrations by Loreen Leedy

When I Count to One
Illustrations by Ann Grifalconi
✳ CALDECOTT HONOR ILLUSTRATOR

One Gorilla
by Atsuko Morozumi

**Little Fish
Froggie, Froggie**
Illustrations by David Diaz

Featured Poets

Dorothy Aldis
Aileen Fisher
David McCord
William Jay Smith

BOOK B
Hurry, Furry Feet

The Foot Book
Hurry, Hurry, Hurry
by Dr. Seuss
✳ CALDECOTT HONOR ILLUSTRATOR

Where Is Bravo?
by Cecilia Avalos

My Street Begins at My House
by Ella Jenkins
Illustrations by
James E. Ransome

The Wheels on the Bus
Traditional Song

When the Elephant Walks
by Keiko Kasza
✳ ALA NOTABLE AUTHOR

Un elefante (One Elephant)
Traditional Latin American Song

Sitting in My Box
by Dee Lillegard
Illustrations by Jon Agee

Featured Poets

Harriet Ziefert
Evelyn Beyer
Dorothy Baruch

BOOK C
Our Singing Planet

"Pardon?" Said the Giraffe
by Colin West

I Can Make Music
by Eve B. Feldman

**Folk Songs from
North and South America**

**The Little Red Hen
and the Grain of Wheat**
by Sara Cone Bryant

Featured Poets

N. M. Bodecker
Rowena Bennett
Mary Ann Hoberman
Lee Bennett Hopkins

My Mom Travels a Lot
by Caroline Feller Bauer
Illustrations by
Nancy Winslow Parker
✹ CHRISTOPHER AWARD
✹ NEW YORK TIMES BEST ILLUSTRATED

Tommy Meng San
by Belinda Yun-Ying
and Douglas Louie

BOOK D
My Favorite Foodles

The Doorbell Rang
by Pat Hutchins
✳ ALA NOTABLE CHILDREN'S BOOK
✳ CHILDREN'S CHOICE

Aiken Drum
Traditional Song

**The Great, Big,
Enormous Turnip**
retold by Alexei Tolstoy
Illustrations by
Helen Oxenbury
✳ ALA NOTABLE ILLUSTRATOR

From Seeds to Zucchinis
by LuLu Delacre

Hello, House!
retold by Linda Hayward
Illustrations by
Lynn Munsinger
✳ NEW YORK TIMES BEST ILLUSTRATOR

THE GREAT BIG
ENORMOUS TURNIP
Pictures by
HELEN OXENBURY
Story by
ALEXEI TOLSTOY

A House Is a House
for Me
MARY ANN HOBERMAN
Illustrated by BETTY FRASER

Featured Poets

Eve Merriam
Lucia and James L. Hymes, Jr.
Dennis Lee
John Ciardi
Mary Ann Hoberman
Charlotte Zolotow

The Doorbell Rang
by Pat Hutchins

BOOK E
Happy Faces

Mouse's Marriage
by Junko Morimoto
✳ AUSTRALIAN PICTURE BOOK
OF THE YEAR ILLUSTRATOR

Who Will Bell the Cat?
retold as a play
by Sandy Asher

Mice
by Rose Fyleman

We Are Little Mice
Somos Unos Ratoncitos
by Frances Alexander

The Mice Go Marching
by Hap Palmer

Mama's Birthday Present
by Carmen Tafolla

Baby Rattlesnake
by TeAta
retold by Lynn Moroney

The Desert
by Carol Carrick
✳ *NEW YORK TIMES* NOTABLE AUTHOR

It's George
by Miriam Cohen
Illustrations by Lillian Hoban
✳ CHRISTOPHER AWARD ILLUSTRATOR

A DELL YOUNG YEARLING
IT'S GEORGE!
Story by Miriam Cohen
Pictures by Lillian Hoban

Nathaniel Talking
by Eloise Greenfield
illustrated by Jan Spivey Gilchrist

Featured Poets

Eloise Greenfield
Alonzo Lopez
Karla Kuskin
Myra Cohn Livingston
Marchette Chute
Kali Grosvenor

BOOK F

A Canary with Hiccups

Two Greedy Bears
retold by Mirra Ginsburg
Illustrations by
Jose Aruego and Ariane Dewey
✳ ALA NOTABLE AUTHOR
✳ BOSTON GLOBE-HORN
BOOK AWARD ILLUSTRATOR

Eat Up, Gemma
by Sarah Hayes
Illustrations by Jan Ormerod
✳ KATE GREENAWAY
AUTHOR/ILLUSTRATOR TEAM AWARD

A Healthy Day
by Paul Showers
✳ NEW JERSEY INSTITUTE OF
TECHNOLOGY AWARD AUTHOR

Looby Loo
Traditional Song

**Henry and Mudge
and the Forever Sea**
from the story by
Cynthia Rylant
Illustrations by Suçie Stevenson
✳ PARENTING READING MAGIC AWARD
✳ NEWBERY MEDAL AUTHOR

Amazing Pets
by Lynda DeWitt

Fox on the Job
from the story by
James Marshall
✳ ALA NOTABLE CHILDREN'S AUTHOR
✳ READING RAINBOW SELECTION

Do Your Ears Hang Low?
Illustrations by Lois Ehlert
✳ ALA NOTABLE ILLUSTRATOR

Ready...Set...Read!
from the book by Joanna Cole
and Stephanie Calmenson
Illustrations by Lois Ehlert

Featured Poets

Jack Prelutsky
Lee Bennett Hopkins
Shel Silverstein
Argentina Palacios
Gail Kredenser
Zheyna Gay

OUR SINGING PLANET

Titles in This Set

⭐

Under My Hat
Hurry, Furry Feet
Our Singing Planet
My Favorite Foodles
Happy Faces
A Canary with Hiccups

About the Cover

An artist named Kiki painted the cover. She was born in Germany, but now lives in a small village in Mexico. This is a peaceful place for her to make her paintings. Kiki likes to draw children. She has three boys of her own.

ISBN: 0-673-80013-X

Acknowledgments appear on page 128.

45678910 VHJ 99989796959493

OUR SINGING PLANET

ScottForesman

A Division of HarperCollins*Publishers*

Contents

Wild Things

"Pardon?" Said the Giraffe   10
Fantasy written and illustrated
by Colin West

A Word from the Author   26
Article by Colin West

Lion   28
Poem by N. M. Bodecker

When You Talk to a Monkey   29
Poem by Rowena Bennett

Abracadabra   30
Poem by Mary Ann Hoberman

I Like Music

I Can Make Music   38
Narrative nonfiction by Eve B. Feldman

Clap Your Hands   46
American folk song

My Farm   47
Argentine folk song

Hambone   48
Traditional African-American song
Illustrations by Buena Johnson

A Word from the Illustrator   52
Article by Buena Johnson

6

Nice Job!

**The Little Red Hen
and the Grain of Wheat**   56
British folk tale retold by Sara Cone Bryant

READ ALONG

My Mom Travels a Lot   78
Realistic fiction by Caroline Feller Bauer

Last Laugh   110
Poem by Lee Bennett Hopkins

This Is the Way We Build a House   111
Song based on "Here We Go 'Round the Mulberry Bush"

Tommy Meng San   112
Realistic fiction by Belinda Yun-Ying and Douglas Louie

A Word from the Authors   120
Article by Belinda Yun-Ying and Douglas Louie

Student Resources
Books to Enjoy   122
Pictionary   124

Wild Things

"PARDON?" SAID THE GIRAFFE

by Colin West

"What's it like up there?"
asked the frog
as he hopped on the ground.

"Pardon?" said
the giraffe.

"What's it like up there?"
asked the frog
as he hopped on the lion.

"Pardon?" said
the giraffe.

"What's it like up there?"
asked the frog
as he hopped on the hippo.

"Pardon?" said
the giraffe.

15

"What's it like up there?"
asked the frog
as he hopped on the elephant.

"Pardon?" said
the giraffe.

"What's it like up there?"
asked the frog

18

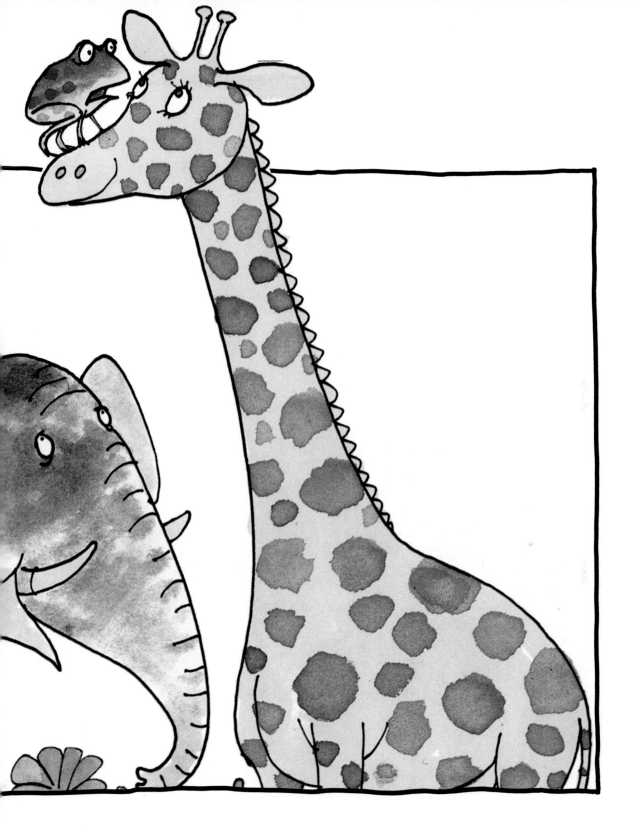

as he hopped on the giraffe.

"It's nice up here, thank you,"
said the giraffe,

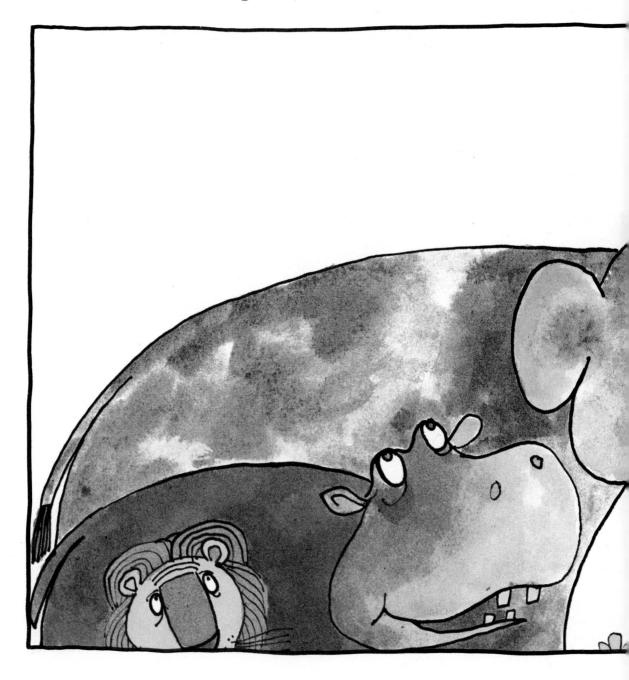

"but you're tickling my nose
and I think I'm going to . . ."

"A-A-A-CHOOOOOOOOO!"

"Ooooops!" said the frog.

"What's it like down there?"
asked the giraffe.

"Pardon?" said the frog.

Tall Talk, Small Talk
by Colin West

You can have fun with the animal voices in my story.

When I read my story aloud, I use a deep voice for the giraffe. I make the word "Pardon?" very long. So, it's "'PAAAAAARDON?' said the giraffe." I make the frog's voice get louder and louder as the story goes along.

Why not try reading the story this way?

I hope you enjoy my story and pictures.

Colin West

Lion

by N. M. Bodecker

The lion,
when he roars
at night,
gives many people
quite
a fright!

The lion,
when he roars
by day,
scares people near him
far
away.

And when
he sleeps,
his lion snore
is quite as scary as
his
roar.

When You Talk to a Monkey

by Rowena Bennett

When you talk to a monkey
   He seems very wise.
He scratches his head,
   And he blinks both his eyes;
But he won't say a word.
   He just swings on a rail
And makes a big question mark
   Out of his tail.

Abracadabra

by Mary Ann Hoberman

GROUP 1:   Abracadabra
            The zebra is black.

GROUP 2:   Abracadabra
            The zebra is white.

30

GROUP 1:   Abracadabra
           The zebra is dark.

GROUP 2:   Abracadabra
           The zebra is light.

GROUP 1: Is it black striped with white?
Is it white striped with black?

GROUP 2:   Is it striped from the front?
Is it striped from the back?

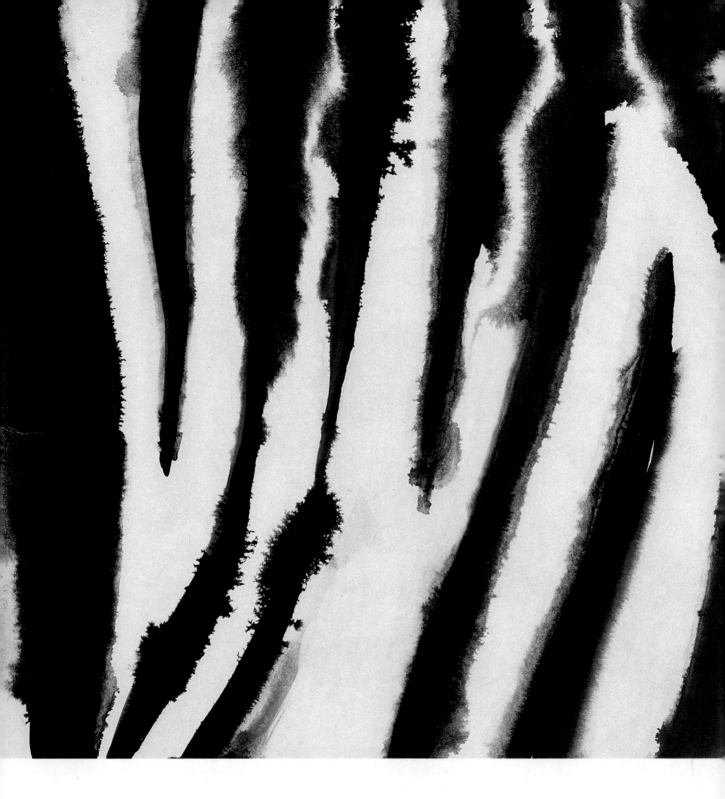

GROUP 1:   Abracadabra
            It's ink over snow.

GROUP 2:   Abracadabra
            It's snow over ink.

ALL: Abracadabra
        Does anyone know?

        Abracadabra
        What do you think?

I Like Music

I Can Make Music!

by Eve B. Feldman

I can make music.

Boom! Tap! Boom!

My hands can tap the beat.

I can make music.

Jangle! Jingle! Jangle!

Bells jingle on my feet.

I can make music.

Toot! Blow! Toot!

Each blow makes a sound.

40

I can make music.

Rattle! Shake! Rattle!

I shake this all around.

I can make music.

Pluck! Strum! Pluck!

My fingers strum the strings.

I can make music.

Ping! Tap! Ping!

I tap and the music rings.

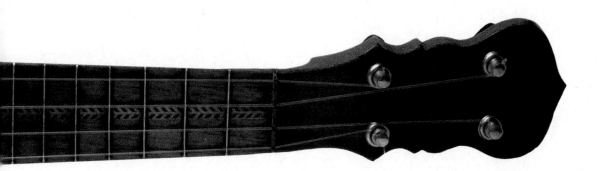

You can make music too!

Try this.

Use a clean and dry container.

Fill it with dry peas, beans, or rice.

Seal it with tape and shake!

Clap Your Hands

Clap, clap, clap your hands,
Clap your hands together.
Clap, clap, clap your hands,
Clap your hands together.

Shake, shake, shake the beat,
Shake the beat together.
Shake, shake, shake the beat,
Shake the beat together.

My Farm

Come now and see my farm, for it is beautiful.
Come now and see my farm, for it is beautiful.
El pollito sounds like this: peep, peep.
El pollito sounds like this: peep, peep.

Come now and see my farm, for it is beautiful.
Come now and see my farm, for it is beautiful.
El gatito sounds like this: meow, meow.
El gatito sounds like this: meow, meow.

Hambone

Adapted by Cheryl Warren Mattox

Illustrations by Buena Johnson

Hambone, Hambone, where you been?
'Round the world and back again!

Hambone, Hambone, have you heard?
Papa's gonna buy me a mockingbird.

If that mockingbird don't sing,
Papa's gonna buy me a diamond ring.

If that diamond ring don't shine,
Papa's gonna buy me a fishing line.

Hambone, Hambone, where you been?
'Round the world and I'm goin' again!

DO HAMBONE AGAIN!

by Buena Johnson

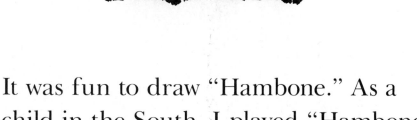

It was fun to draw "Hambone." As a child in the South, I played "Hambone" as a game.

I remember an old man I used to call Uncle. Uncle would sing "Hambone" and pat out a beat on his legs. I never got tired of hearing him. I would ask him over and over, "Uncle, can you do 'Hambone' again?"

However you play and sing "Hambone," you can keep the fun going on and on.

Buena Johnson

Nice Job!

The Little Red Hen and the Grain of Wheat

Retold by Sara Cone Bryant

One day as the Little Red Hen was
scratching in a field, she found a
grain of wheat.

"This wheat should be planted," she said.
"Who will plant this grain of wheat?"

"Not I," said the Duck.
"Not I," said the Cat.
"Not I," said the Dog.

"Then I will," said the Little Red Hen.
And she did.

Soon the wheat grew to be tall
and yellow.

"The wheat is ripe," said the Little Red Hen.
"Who will cut the wheat?"

"Not I," said the Duck.
"Not I," said the Cat.
"Not I," said the Dog.

"Then I will," said the Little Red Hen.
And she did.

When the wheat was cut, the Little Red Hen
said, "Who will thresh this wheat?"

"Not I," said the Duck.
"Not I," said the Cat.
"Not I," said the Dog.

"Then I will," said the Little Red Hen.
And she did.

When the wheat was all threshed, the Little
Red Hen said, "Who will take this wheat to
the mill?"

"Not I," said the Duck.
"Not I," said the Cat.
"Not I," said the Dog.

"Then I will," said the Little Red Hen.
And she did.

She took the wheat to the mill and had it
ground into flour.

Then she said, "Who will make this
flour into bread?"

"Not I," said the Duck.

"Not I," said the Cat.

"Not I," said the Dog.

"Then I will," said the Little Red Hen.
And she did.

She made and baked the bread.

Then she said, "Who will eat this bread?"

"Oh! I will," said the Duck.
"And I will," said the Cat.
"And I will," said the Dog.

"No, no!" said the Little Red Hen. "I will do that."

And she did.

MY MOM TRAVELS A LOT

by

CAROLINE FELLER BAUER

Illustrations by

NANCY WINSLOW PARKER

My mom travels a lot.

The good thing about it is
we get to go to the airport.

The bad thing about it is
there's only one nighttime kiss.

The bad thing about it is
Mom wasn't home when Susie
had her puppies.

The good thing about it is
we get lots of postcards.

The bad
thing
about it is
Mom
missed
the school
play.

The good thing about it is
Dad and I eat out more often.

The bad thing about it is
I always forget to water
the plants.

The good thing about it is
I don't always have to make
my bed.

The bad thing about it is
Dad can never find my boots.

The good thing about it is
sometimes I get to stay
up late.

The bad thing about it is
we miss her.

The good thing about it is
we get presents.

But the best thing about it is

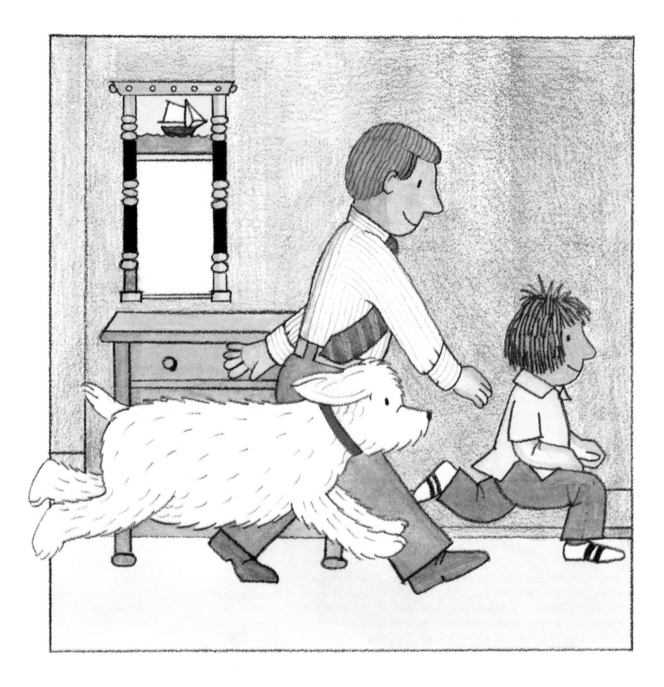

she always comes back!

Last Laugh

by Lee Bennett Hopkins

They all laughed when I told them
I wanted to be

A woman in space
Floating so free.

But they won't laugh at me
When they finally see
My feet up on Mars
And my face on TV.

This Is the Way We Build a House

This is the way we build a house,
  build a house, build a house.
This is the way we build a house,
  as we work all day.

This is the way we saw the wood,
  saw the wood, saw the wood.
This is the way we saw the wood,
  as we work all day.

This is the way we hammer the nails,
  hammer the nails, hammer the nails.
This is the way we hammer the nails,
  as we work all day.

Tommy Meng San

by Belinda Yun-Ying and Douglas Louie

Tommy ran into the house.
"We had a call from Hong Kong," said Father.
"Grandmother fell and hurt her leg.
She is coming to stay with us."

"Baba, what can I do to make Grandmother
feel better?" asked Tommy.
"You can make her a card," said Father.
"I know that will help her feel better."

Tommy made his card.
Then he began to write his name.
He stopped.

"Grandmother calls me Meng San.
She'll like it if I write my Chinese
name," he thought.

114

"Baba, can you teach me to write
Meng San?" Tommy asked.

Father showed him the strokes.
Father said, "The first word, Meng,
means bright.
It looks like the sun and the moon."

"The second word is San.
It means mountain.
The word looks like a mountain too.
We want you to grow up to be as strong
as a mountain."

Tommy wrote his name on the card.
He was very proud.

Just then, Tommy's cat jumped on the table.

"Get down!" Tommy yelled.

Too late. Little San walked over Tommy's words.

"Little San, you spoiled my card.
Now what will I do?" Tommy said.

He had an idea.

"Baba, can you teach me to write my cat's name?" said Tommy.

Father showed him the Chinese words for Little San.
Tommy wrote his cat's name above his own name.
"Now the card is from both of us," he said.

118

The day came for Grandmother's visit.
Tommy gave the card to Grandmother.

"Thank you, Meng San," said Grandmother.
"And thank you, Little San," she said
with a big smile.

119

Do Your Best

by Belinda Yun-Ying and Douglas Louie

We live in Seattle, Washington, with our two small children, Philip and Andrea.

We always tell our children to do their best. Our story shows how children can be proud of their work.

We hope our story will make you want to do your best too.

Belinda Yun Ying Louie

雷吳潤瑛

Douglas Louie

雷向榮

Books to Enjoy

"Not Me," Said the Monkey
by Colin West

Someone is making trouble
in the jungle. Who could
it be? Is it you?

Caps for Sale
by Esphyr Slobodkina

A peddler walks with a huge
stack of caps on his head.
One day he stops to take a
nap under a tree. Look
out, peddler, there are
monkeys in the tree!

Party Rhymes
by Marc Brown

Do you know "Skip to My Lou"
and "The Farmer in the Dell"?
Here's a book you can read
and sing.

Baby Beluga

by Raffi

Illustrations by Ashley Wolff

Read this song about a baby beluga whale. Find out where he swims and who his friends are.

Who Is the Beast?

by Keith Baker

Does a beast have a long tail, white whiskers, and green eyes? What do <u>you</u> think?

Daddies at Work

by Eve Merriam

Illustrations by Eugenie Fernandes

Daddies lift you up. Daddies sing silly songs. Daddies fix broken toys. Daddies are busy people.

Pictionary

police officer

mail carrier

HOSPITAL

LIBRARY

doctor

librarian

124

pilot

musician

farmer

cook

teacher

bear
frog

Where Things Are

behind

in front of

on

under

Acknowledgments

Text

Page 10: *''Pardon?'' Said the Giraffe* by Colin West. Copyright © 1986 by Colin West. Reprinted by permission of HarperCollins Publishers and Walker Books Limited.

Page 26: ''Tall Talk, Small Talk'' by Colin West. Copyright © 1991 by Colin West.

Page 28: ''Lion'' by N. M. Bodecker. Used with permission of Margaret K. McElderry Books, an imprint of Macmillan Publishing Company, from *Snowman Sniffles and Other Verse,* written and illustrated by N. M. Bodecker. Copyright © 1983 by N. M. Bodecker.

Page 29: ''When You Talk to a Monkey'' from *The Day Is Dancing* by Rowena Bennett. Copyright © 1948, © 1968 by Rowena Bennett. Reprinted by permission of Modern Curriculum Press.

Page 30: ''Abracadabra'' from *A Fine Fat Pig and Other Animal Poems* by Mary Ann Hoberman. Text copyright © 1991 by Mary Ann Hoberman. Reprinted by permission of HarperCollins Publishers.

Page 38: *I Can Make Music* by Eve Feldman. Copyright © 1991 by Eve Feldman.

Page 46: ''Clap Your Hands'' by Charles Seeger from *American Folk Songs for Children* by Ruth Crawford Seeger. Copyright © 1948 by Ruth Crawford Seeger. Reprinted by permission of Michael Seeger, Co-executor, Estate of Charles and Ruth Seeger.

Page 48: ''Hambone.'' Arrangement by Cheryl Warren Mattox from *Shake It to the One That You Love the Best.* Copyright © 1989 by Warren Mattox Productions. Reprinted by permission of Warren Mattox Productions.

Page 52: ''Play 'Hambone' Again'' by Buena Johnson. Copyright © 1991 by Buena Johnson.

Page 56: *The Little Red Hen and the Grain of Wheat* retold by Sara Cone Bryant, *Stories to Tell to Children.* Boston: Houghton Mifflin Company.

Page 78: *My Mom Travels a Lot* by Caroline Feller Bauer. Text Copyright © 1981 by Caroline Feller Bauer. Illustrations Copyright © 1981 by Nancy Winslow Parker. Used by permission of Viking Penguin, a division of Penguin Books USA Inc.

Page 110: ''Last Laugh'' from *Kim's Place and Other Poems* by Lee Bennett Hopkins. Copyright © 1974 by Lee Bennett Hopkins. Reprinted by permission of Curtis Brown Ltd.

Page 112: *Tommy Meng San* by Belinda Yun-Ying and Douglas Louie. Copyright 1991 by Belinda Yun-Ying and Douglas Louie.

Page 120: ''Do Your Best'' by Belinda Yun-Ying and Douglas Louie. Copyright © 1991 by Belinda Yun-Ying and Douglas Louie.

Artists

Illustrations owned and copyrighted by the illustrator.
Kiki Suarez, 1–9, 36–37, 54–55, 122–127
Colin West, 10–26
N. M. Bodecker, 28
Chris Demarest, 29
Helen Cowcher, 30–35
Susan Spellman, 38–45
Beatriz Vidal, 46–47
Buena Johnson, 48–53
Don Almquist, 56–77
Nancy Winslow Parker, 78–109
Joe Van Der Bos, 110–111
Mike Reed, 112–121

Freelance Photography

Photographs not listed were shot by Scott, Foresman and Company.

Photographs

Page 52: Courtesy of Buena Johnson.
Page 120: Courtesy of Belinda Yun-Ying and Douglas Louie.